Ricky Roogle

THE GRILLED BOOK

Jokes and cartoons about barbecue

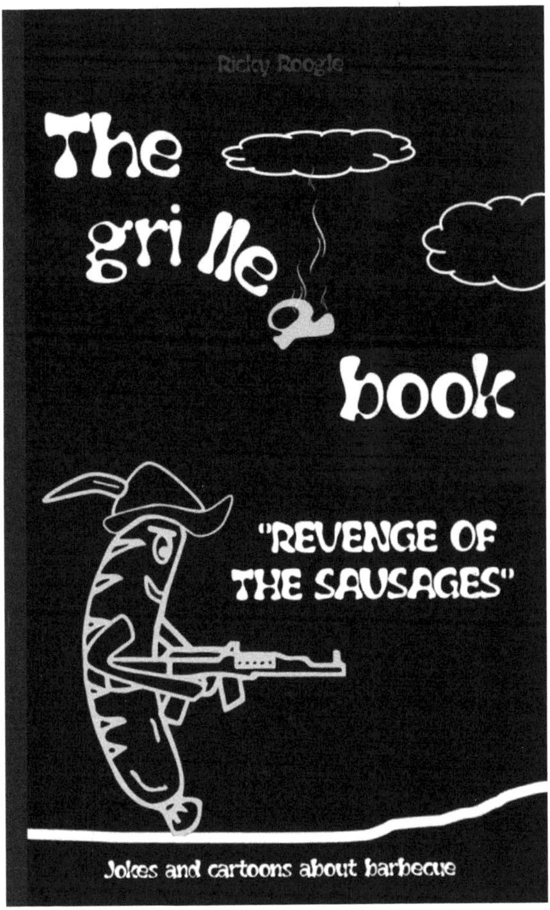

A short history of this book.

Bibliographic information of the German National Library: The German National Library lists this publication in the German National Bibliography; detailed bibliographic data are available on the Internet at http://dnb.dnb.de.

© 2022 Ricky Roogle; 1st edition
Cover art, text & illustrations © 2022 Ricky Roogle
Author contact: ricky.roogle@t-online.de
Production and publishing: BoD – Books on Demand, Norderstedt
ISBN: 9783756224449

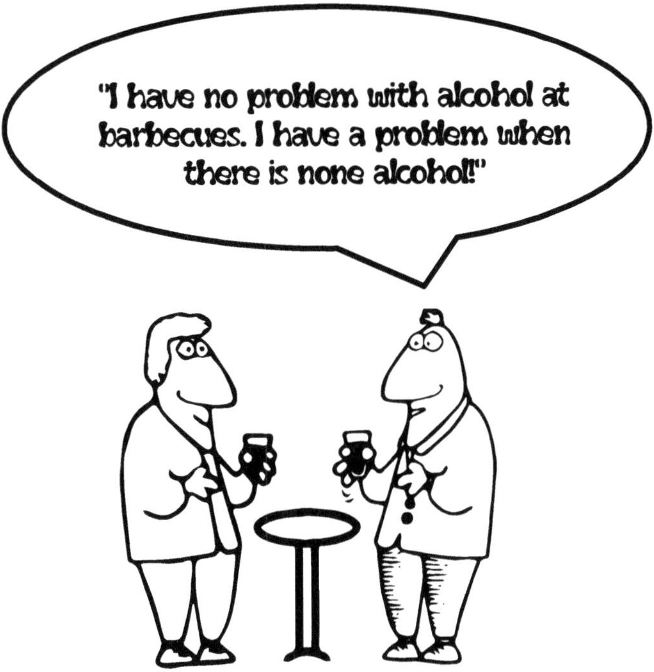

Effects of a barbecue evening

If there is one sheep less to count before you go to sleep, that was me. I had lamb today.

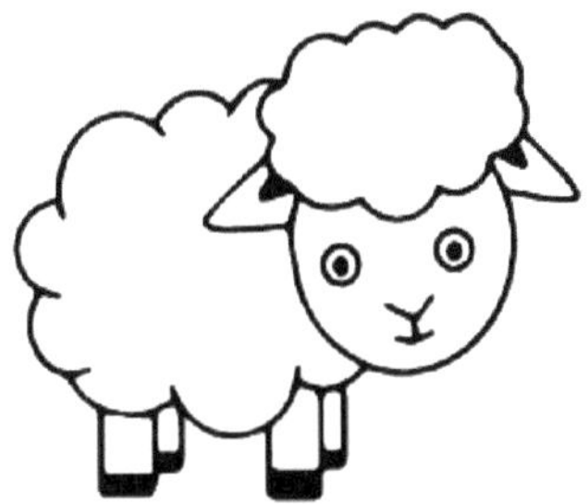

Thanks for the barbecue plate! Was able to discover the steak in the end!

AT THE BARBECUE PARTY

THE MAIN THING IS A GOOD BARBECUE

"The steak resembles a piece of coal, more than anything else!"

"But it has an undisputable advantage."

"Which one?"

"The calories have all been burnt!"

PLANET OF THE SAUSAGES

BRATWURST CAESAR IS HUNTING THE
LAST HUMANS.

SHOPPING LIST FOR BARBECUE EVENING

Woman:	Man:
- salad	- meat
- wine	- beer
- dips	
- herb butter	
- cheese cubes	
- napkins	
- ketchup	
- mayonnaise	
- potatoes	
- peppers	
- pepperoni	
- cucumbers	
- bread	
- corn on the cob	
- crème fraîche	
- tomatoes	
- onions	
- olives	
- coke	
- sprite	

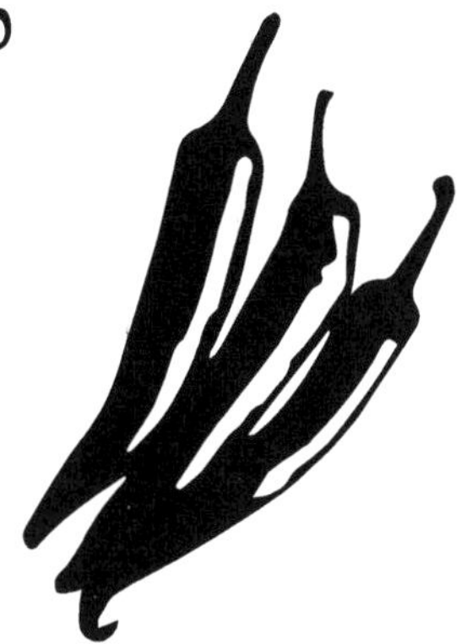

If you want to barbecue and
then you see this sign...

In the old days, 30 years ago, at a
barbecue, the first question was,
"What do you have to drink?"
Today, at a barbecue, the first
question is: "Can someone tell me
the Wi-Fi password?"

What other name is there among
barbecue lovers for 'barbecue night'?

Meating Point

To all vegetarians. There is a reason why
one speaks of vegging out and not of
slaughtering away.

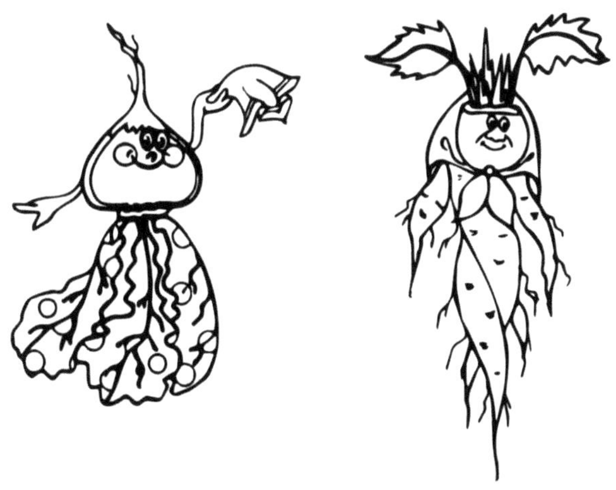

In the South Seas. A large luxury liner has sunk. A man escaped the sinking ship in time and reaches the saving shore. Two cannibals catch him, tie him to a spit and grill the shipwrecked man over the campfire. Says one:

I asked a supermarket clerk the other day where I could find the barbecue lighters, he replied:

"Daily papers are to the right of the tills."

Star Wurst, the vegan menace.

Cleopatra (vegetarian) messes up the barbecue evening
"For the barbecue, your subjects want to grill ten oxen. No one wants to eat the vegetables."
"Nope!"

Couldn't eat meat any more.

Bang! Extinct!

The other day in the South Seas

Star Wurst

BARBECUE DATE

"You're a barbecue expert, which wine do you recommend to go with a barbecue?"
"Beer."
Am I against vegetables? No, nothing at all, I want my food to be healthy!

"Why do you like being invited to barbecues so much?"
"That's because I'm small and delicate. And then, when I join the BBQ, I eat up 10 sausages, 4 steaks and all the potato salad."

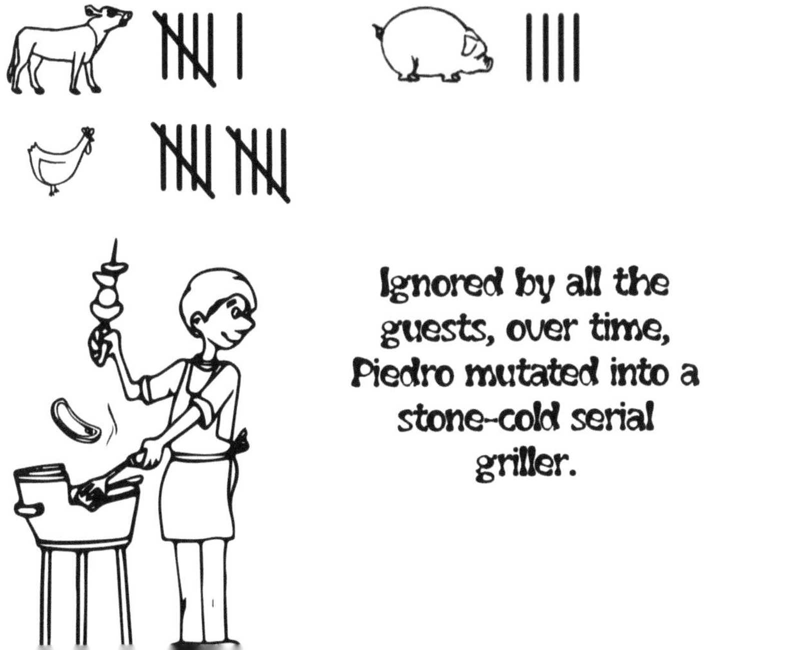

Ignored by all the guests, over time, Piedro mutated into a stone-cold serial griller.

"What kind of pathetic grill is that? You can't have more than two steaks?"
"That's because it's a toaster, Kevin!"

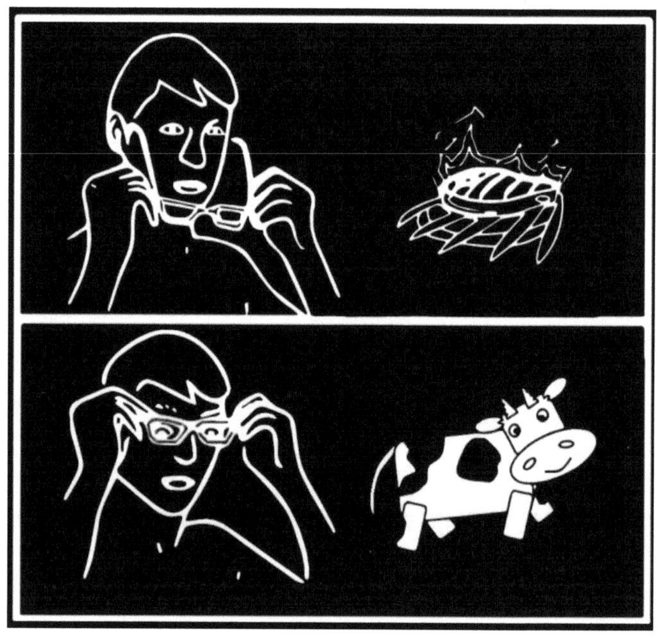

"Tonight, we're having a barbecue."

5213 wasps liked it.
14131 wasps have commented on this event.
756 wasps have shared the event.
3 wasps invite to a "disturbing action at Homo Sapiens".
605 wasps want to participate.

Moses, a self-convinced barbecue fan, extended the ten commandments

A father-son conversation

How you feel when you succeed as a barbecue chef in not letting anything burn for the whole barbecue evening.

"I am God."

Another stunning aesthetic advantage when eating meat:

Meat does not crumble.

We're barbecuing now (,) Grandpa!
(Punctuation marks can save lives!)

Now, it is finally clear, how vegans
reproduce.
They don't have children, they
produce sprouts.

And Moses spoke:
"I have had expensive steaks burnt on the grill",
and the sea thus:

Crematorium for barbecue fans

Barbecue is happiness.

Now it's the time of year again, when the supermarket offers road salt and barbecue charcoal at the same time.

Again and again, the grilling process is compared to sex. Is this so? Judge for yourself based on the following statements:

- If you don't clean up properly downstairs, it may burn.

- Did you invite the neighbours?

- Your sausage looks wrinkly.

- If you carry on like this, the neighbours will complain again.

- Look, it's really amazing, how the juice runs out.

- Wait until the sauce comes, then, it's perfect.

- If the piece is too dry, I can't enjoy it.

- You still have something on your mouth.

- A little blood is okay.

- We could actually do this more often.

- It's not ready, yet, it has to put on again!

- Three minutes or well done?

- Now, we turn the tables!

- My wife loves my meat in her mouth.

A grill master is confronted with the question about life after death:

"Where do I want to be when I'm dead?"

When the food is smarter than the grill master

Grill master: "Anyone for the sausage with the dark side?"

"Are we still on for the barbecue tonight?"

"But it's raining so heavily all the time."

"Well, it's only fish then."

When you've bought loads of meat and sausages for a barbecue with friends and then it rains heavily for weeks on end.

When a distant acquaintance comes
along for a barbecue....

and it turns out, he's a
vegan...

When you are in a coma,

and you finally wake up
after 20 years,

and your first question to the doctor is:
"Are the boys having another barbecue tonight?"

Everyone is outraged that the world is
getting more and more out of whack!
Then you go to the discount store
buy a package of 5 chops for $2.49
and go to a barbecue.

Chops today

"So what's your fitness plan for today?"

"I'm concentrating on my stomach and neck"

"Great, so I'll see you at the gym later?"

"There's a grill there?"

"The Millers have invited me to a
barbecue this afternoon. They want me
to bring something vegetarian. Thought
of a box of cigarettes."

"Why are hamburgers so happy at barbecues?"
"Don't know. Why?"
"They will meet all their old flames."

Why is Chuck Norris the best barbecue master?
He can grill under water.

ATTENTION EXTREME GRILLERS!

"That's it for the barbecue today."
"Why?"
"I think Frank got the part about deglazing the meat wrong."

"How about a barbecue today? Please
bring beer, coal, the grill and the meat.
I'll take care of the cutlery."

My contribution:

"Well, it looks like you're
barbecuing again, today?"
"But no, I'm just preparing the
three-legged top bowl to
sacrifice curious, stupidly
questioning neighbours to the
goddess Grilla."

"O great Grilla!
Accept my sacrifice!"

"It used to be my greatest wish doing something with animals when I grew up. That's the reason, why I like grilling so much now!"

formerly today

Grill rule no.1:
It is not possible to use too much garlic!

What are the four seasons called from a griller's point of view?

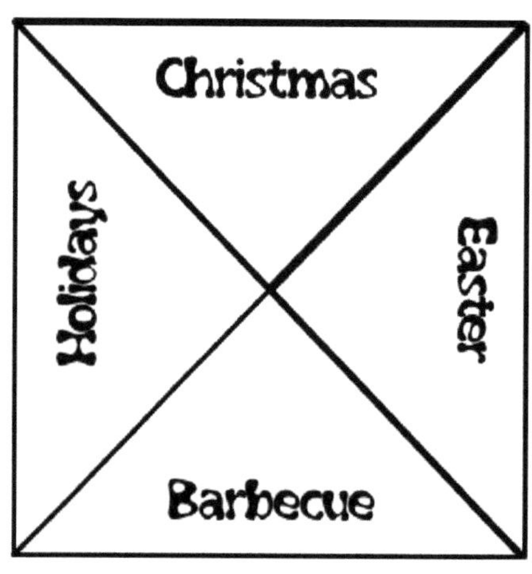

The police come to the Millers'
garden, who are having a barbecue.
A man with a knife in his back is lying
on the grass next to the barbecue.
The policeman turns to the grill
master and asks:

What do I eat at the barbecue?
Potato salad, mixed salad, baguette ...
until something is ready from the grill.

What upsets me? My neighbours.
They buy high tech grill for $900
and then grill a cheap 99 Cent
packet of 10 sausages.

In the South Seas. A luxury steamer
has sunk.
With the last of his strength the
clown of the steamer's theatre group
reaches the beach of an island.
Two cannibals find the exhausted
man. They throw him into a huge pot
and cook him over the campfire.
Then, one of the cannibals tastes him
and says:

The different types of headache

Migraine

Hypertension

Stress

**Someone has ignored
the ban on vegetables
for the barbecue!**

Do you know what I mean?
The time, when you can't
barbecue?
And you don't know, what to do
with your life?

What there should be

My friends think I'm addicted to
barbecues. But I always make
sure to balance my time
according to importance.

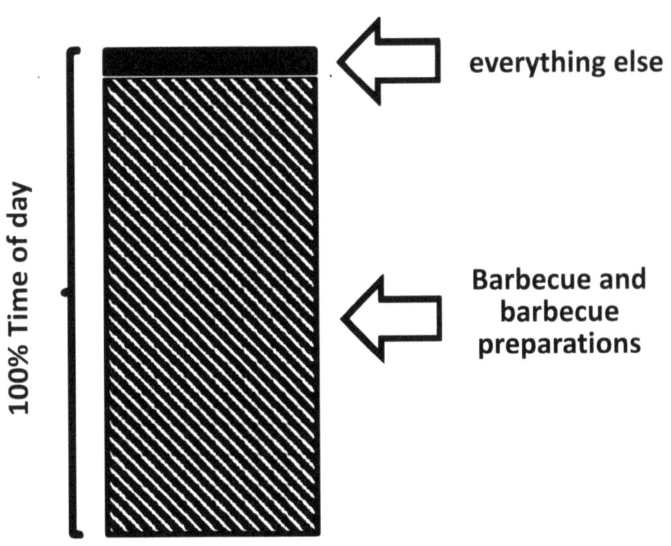

Summer, five o'clock in the afternoon:
"Yay, closing time! What do we want to do now? Go for a swim? Walk to the ice cream parlour? Go for a walk in the forest? Have a barbecue?"
Winter, five o'clock in the afternoon:
"Gloomy, hazy, dark. I'm going to sleep."

"Do you fancy a barbecue in my garden tonight?"
"Is it covered?"
"No, it's a spontaneous idea."

Stupid Aliens

"Hey guys, dead end. The dominant life form is still in too primitive a phase of life. They have only just discovered fire and are still grilling their food!"

The thing that vegetarians just don't want to understand. If God had wanted us not to eat animals, why did he make them of meat?

Where does Chuck Norris go to barbecue?
He goes to the sun. Anything else would
be too cold for him.

The grill master opens the barbecue:
"Welcome to this barbecue!
Since we also have vegans among the guests this time, I would like to point out that the cold buffet is over there!"
"Do you mean the compost heap?"
"Cold buffet!"

What does the mafiosi at the barbecue say:
"If I may introduce myself, Luigi, mission griller."

What do you call it when
vegans have sex with each
other?

They reproduce.

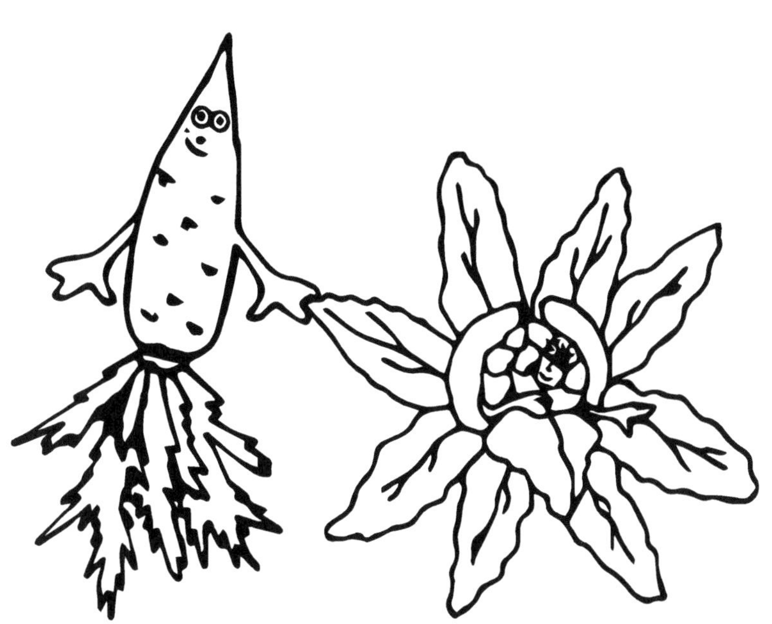

The barbecue elf

Stock photo

People can basically be divided into two categories based on their eating habits:

Category 1: Only eat certain food at set times.

Category 2: "Leftovers from the barbecue and cake from Sunday for breakfast? Awesome! Bring it on!"

And then there are
always those, who
cannot separate work
and private life.

Everyone talks about the need for more innovation in our country. I have an idea. How about, if the sat nav would not only show the petrol stations, but also the locations of the trucks with grilled chicken?

Wow! The unsuspecting neighbour is just starting to fire up his barbecue!
That means, waiting exactly 45 minutes, then going over to him with sad, longing eyes and bringing him back his snow shovel from last December.

Why does the grill master hold a
minute's silence at the grill?
It is the minute of shame for not having
killed the animal himself.

How do you find out,
that a vegan is at the
barbecue?
He tells you.

The very rare and shy steak fish

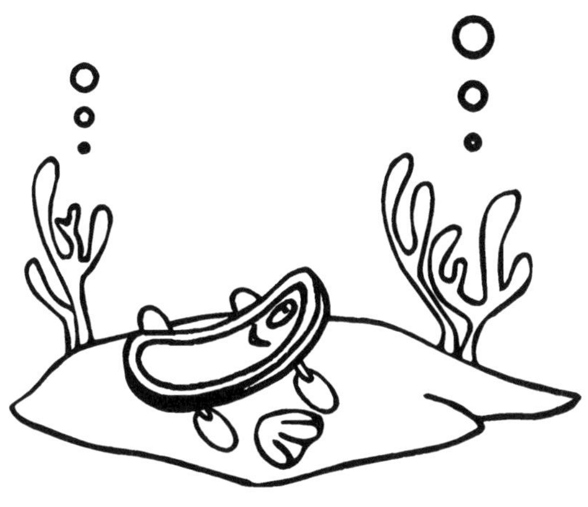

One barbecue master to another:
"Now it's scientifically proven why men like
to barbecue so much."
"And what's the reason?"
"Because chopping lettuce sucks!"

The Baker family is having a barbecue.
Suddenly Father Christmas joins them on
the terrace and says:
"Ho! Ho! Ho! Merry Christmas. And sorry,
I'm late, but my sleigh broke down and
two of my reindeer are sick, so I had to
walk."

No, grilled meat is not fattening. Drinking
beer while waiting for the meat to be
ready is fattening.

Eat vegetables?
We have not reached the top of the
food chain to be relegated to a
vegetarian.

World premiere of 'Beauty and the Beast'
For barbecue fans it's:

"Beauty and the Beef"

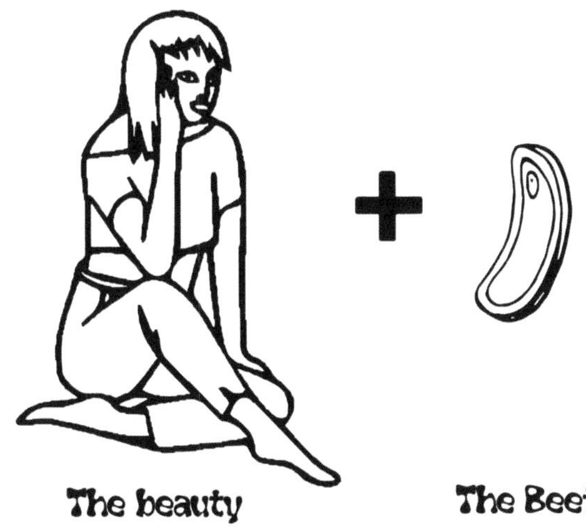

The beauty   The Beef

"Where does the word 'vegetarian'
actually come from?"
"Vegetarian derives from the Indian
language and means 'bad hunter'."

"Tonight at the barbecue, we're having a
real seven-course men's meal."
"What do you mean?"
"Steak and six-pack."

Don't expect anything meaningful from this book. It is packed with lots of absurd and impossible riddles, twisted cartoons and jokes, and paradox scenarios that will shake the reader's worldview.
Buckle up for a mindbending rollercoaster ride through the mind.

"Well done, gnome. This book is grilled completely, but funny."
"Thank you, master Roogle."
If you liked the book, I would appreciate a positive review.
End